A Big Rig

by Melissa Gressok
illustrated by Hector Borlasca

Practice Decodable 23

McGraw Hill Education

Bothell, WA • Chicago, IL • Columbus, OH • New York, NY

MHEonline.com

McGraw Hill Education

Send all inquiries to:
McGraw-Hill Education
8787 Orion Place
Columbus, OH 43240

ISBN: 978-0-02-145306-1
MHID: 0-02-145306-3

Printed in China

8 9 10 11 12 DSS 27 26 25 24 23

Kip spots a big rig.

A big rig lifts up bricks.

A big rig blocks traffic!

Kip had a plan. "Dot! Call Scott."

"A big pig stops traffic?" asks Scott.

Kip and Dot grin. "A big rig!"